THE BIG BOOK OF MOTORBIKES

By Rennie Scaysbrook
Design by Asim Hussain

For my little rider, Harvey.

Contents

Safety

Before every ride, we need to gear up!
That means we wear our helmets, gloves, and protective gear at all times, just like Sarah and Simon.
Wearing the right protective clothing is the best way to stay healthy while we ride. That means we can come back again and again because riding is so much fun!

We love motorbikes because...

A motorbike is one of the best forms of transport.
They're super fun to ride, very interesting to work on, they provide jobs and careers, and help bring people together from all over the world!

MOTORBIKES

It does not matter if you're a girl, a boy, are tall, short, have a disability, or even if you're very young or very old, motorbikes provide fun everyone can enjoy!

Motorbikes can have more than two wheels. Sometimes, they have three wheels, and we call these bikes trikes or sidecars. Sidecars are so much fun, even dogs like to ride in them!

There are many different types of motorbikes. Some are for riding on the street, some are good for riding in the country or in the desert, and some are made for competition!

A person who works on motorbikes for a living is called a mechanic. This is a very technical job they need to study for because keeping a customer's motorbike happy and healthy is a big responsibility.

Motorbikes are amazing tools that can take you all over the world! There's no limit to how far you can ride on a bike and the places you can visit. You'll meet some incredible people along the ride and bring back stories that will last a lifetime.

Motorbike sport is some of the most exciting you can imagine! Big crowds, an incredible atmosphere and some of the most impressive athletes you've ever seen, motorbike sport really gets the blood pumping!

The world is going electric and motorbikes are no different.

An electric motorbike is unique because it is powered by stored electricity! Electric bikes use batteries instead of petrol to help them move, and to "top up the tank" you just plug the bike into an electrical socket like you would with a phone!

Zero Motorcycles were one of the first companies to sell electric motorbikes. Their first bike was called the Zero S and it was sold in 2009. Zero now make electric motorbikes for sale all over the world.

Harley-Davidson released its first electric motorbike in 2019 called the LiveWire! The LiveWire is very different from any bike the company has made before and is almost silent when you ride it. LiveWire is now a brand all its own that was launched in 2021.

The fastest speed record an electric motorbike has reached is 228.05 mph (408 km/h)! Italian legend Max Biaggi rode his Voxan Wattman to that record speed at the Chateauroux airfield in France on October 31, 2020.

Italian brand Energica currently makes the motorbikes for the MotoE World Cup. The MotoE World Cup is the world championship for electric motorbikes!

The longest ride on an electric motorbike was completed by Italian Nicola Colombo in 2013. He rode 7691 miles (12,379 km) across 11 countries from Shanghai in China to Milan in Italy! It took him 13 days to complete his ride.

A very special electric motorbike is the Lightning LS-218 Superbike! This bike was raced by the great Carlin Dunne, who won America's Race To The Clouds, the Pikes Peak International Hill Climb, in 2013. Carlin was so fast on his #5 LS-218, you might even say he was lightning fast!

Motorbike manufacturers are like football teams. They all have their favorite color!

Orange is the color of Austrian motorbike company, KTM. KTM is also the largest European motorbike manufacturer in terms of motorbikes produced each year!

Japan's Kawasaki is famous for the color green. Kawasaki is one of the biggest motorbike companies in the world!

Ducati is famous for producing beautiful red Italian motorbikes, while Japan's Honda is the biggest motorbike company in the world. Italy's Aprilia and MV Agusta also use red in their colors.

Made in Japan, Suzuki motorbikes, especially their dirt bikes, have been yellow for decades. No one else makes yellow bikes because everyone knows yellow is for Suzuki!

Blue is shared by three motorbike companies: Japanese company Yamaha, British company Triumph and German company BMW! Triumph made its first bike in 1902, BMW made its first bike in 1925, and Yamaha made its first bike in 1955.

TRIUMPH

YAMAHA

Black and orange belongs to the one and only Harley-Davidson! This is America's most famous motorbike company, and their headquarters are located in Milwaukee, USA.

Indian Motorcycle use maroon for their color. Indian Motorcycle is America's oldest motorbike company. They started making bikes way back in 1901.

Black is used for Zero Motorcycles! Zero makes electric motorbikes from their base in California!

There are so many cool facts about motorbike history.

Here are just a few!

The first petrol-powered motorbike was the Daimler Reitwagen. It was made in Germany way back in 1885 by Gottlieb Daimler.

Harley-Davidson's first V-twin motorbike was made available to the public in 1909. It was called the Model 5-D.

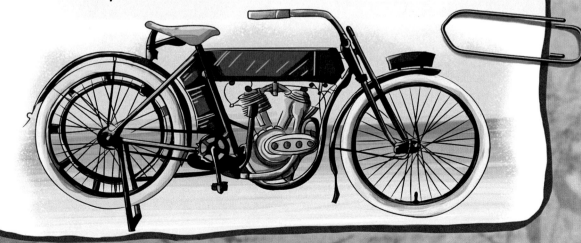

The oldest motorbike brand in the world that has never stopped production is Royal Enfield! Royal Enfield started at the turn of the last century in 1901. That's two years before Harley-Davidson. Royal Enfield was originally from Great Britain, but is now Indian owned.

Yamaha make motorbikes but they also make something else. Yamaha make musical instruments! A piano was their first instrument, and now Yamaha make everything from dirt bikes to stereos and even saxophones!

Honda are so big, they have made over 400 million motorbikes for sale across the world since they first started in 1949!

We know Suzuki make cars and motorbikes, but they didn't start out that way. Before cars and motorbikes, Suzuki used to make weaving equipment for the Japanese silk industry! Back in 1909, the company was called Suzuki Loom Works.

If you go to Italy, you will likely see lots of scooters! Scooters provide a cheap and reliable form of transport, and the most famous scooter manufacturer of them all is the Italian brand, Vespa!

Kawasaki make many things other than motorbikes. Kawasaki Heavy Industries is a very big Japanese company that produces motorbikes, ships, electronics, construction equipment, tractors, trains, helicopters, jet engines, missiles and even space rockets!

Motorbikes can also be used for competition! Motorbike sport comes in many different forms and captivates fans around the world.

Road racing is one of the fastest forms of motorbike competition! Road racing is held on closed asphalt courses, with the very top level being the Grand Prix series that holds races all over the world from the USA to Japan, Europe, Argentina and Australia.

Trials is a very intricate form of competition. Trials riders are some of the most incredible in the world. They ride up things many people would think impossible like rock formations, logs, even little waterfalls!

The oldest motorbike race in the world is the Isle of Man TT! The race was first held in 1907. The Isle of Man TT is held on a 37.73-mile (60.72 km) street course that winds through towns, past schools and over a mountain.

Both motocross and supercross share many similarities, but motocross is held on natural, outdoor tracks like Glen Helen in America and Lommel in Belgium. Supercross is held on man-made indoor tracks, usually at night, inside baseball or football stadiums.

The toughest race in the world is the Dakar Rally!
The Dakar Rally is held over two grueling weeks,
and tests the rider and machine to their limits.
The Dakar Rally has been held in Africa,
South America and Saudi Arabia, taking in some
of the most breathtaking views imaginable.

There's one form of racing where the bikes have no brakes at all.
That's speedway! Speedway races are held over four intense
laps where riders reach speeds of over 80 mph
(128 km/h) with no brakes to slow them down!

Drag racing is where two motorbikes line up side by side and race a quarter mile! Drag racing is a spectacular form of motorbike sport, with super high speeds and very fast reaction times that require the rider to be extremely precise.

Flat track racing is massive all over the world but its heart is in the USA! That's where riders race on spectacular mile-long circuits, inches from each other at over 100 mph (160 km/h).

Motorbikes can be used to set some pretty impressive records, like jumps, wheelies, even lots of people!

Robbie Maddison is a famous Australian daredevil, and he holds the world record for the longest distance jumped on a motorbike from a ramp. The jump distance was an incredible 351 ft (107 meters) in Melbourne, Australia, back in 2008!

WORLD RECORD

There are many famous women in motorbike racing, but there's only one Queen of Rally. The Queen of Rally is none other than Spanish off-road legend, Laia Sanz! Sanz is a World Champion in Trials competition and has competed in and finished an incredible 11 Dakar Rallies.

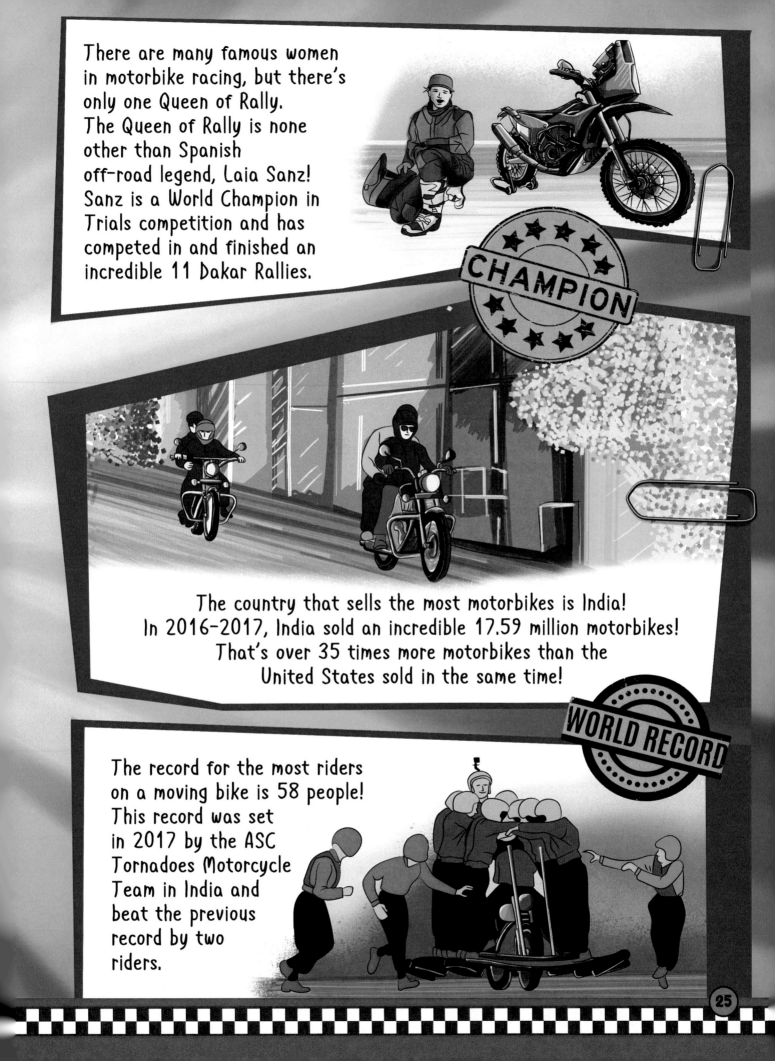

CHAMPION

The country that sells the most motorbikes is India! In 2016-2017, India sold an incredible 17.59 million motorbikes! That's over 35 times more motorbikes than the United States sold in the same time!

WORLD RECORD

The record for the most riders on a moving bike is 58 people! This record was set in 2017 by the ASC Tornadoes Motorcycle Team in India and beat the previous record by two riders.

The highest point anyone has ridden a motorbike is 21,476 feet (6546 meters) above sea level! Swiss rider Jiri Zak rode his motorbike to that height in 2020! Zak was riding on the Ojos del Salado in the South American country of Chile, which is the highest active volcano in the world!

WORLD RECORD

Motorbikes and a tightrope?
You bet!
The man who holds the record for the longest tightrope motorbike ride is Moroccan Mustafa Danger!
Mustafa rode on a steel cable for 426 feet (130 meters) in Spain, in 2010.

The record for the longest journey in a single country belongs to Indian rider Gaurav Siddharth! He rode his Hero Impulse through his home country for 71,708 miles (115,093 km), completing his ride in 2017. In total, Gaurav rode for 588 days, or one year, seven months and 10 days.

American rider Cecil "Bubba" Myers holds the record for the fastest ice wheelie! Cecil rode a Kawasaki on the back wheel on ice to a speed of 132 mph (212.43 km/h) in Wisconsin, USA, in 2017.

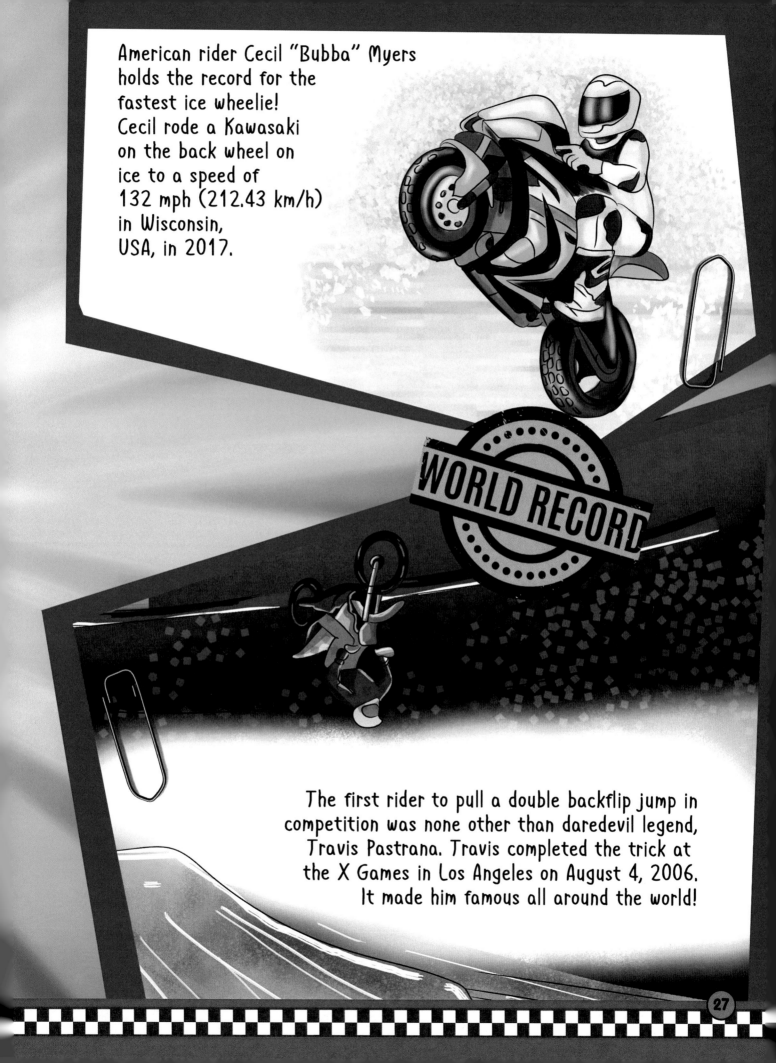

WORLD RECORD

The first rider to pull a double backflip jump in competition was none other than daredevil legend, Travis Pastrana. Travis completed the trick at the X Games in Los Angeles on August 4, 2006. It made him famous all around the world!

Did you enjoy the ride?

"I hope you enjoyed this BIG book about motorbikes, my favorite subject in the whole wide world.

Motorbikes are wonderful social tools that open up so many possibilities in life. Now it's time to get out there and go for a ride—probably after you wake up tomorrow morning!

Rennie Scaysbrook